The titles by which ⦂
to which reference is made in the text, are the Church's
expression of his unique dignity, and our confidence in
his intercession. They include:

Husband of the Blessed Virgin Mary, Guardian of the
Child Jesus and our Redeemer, Head of the Holy Family,
Patron and Protector of the Universal Church; the first of
Patrons, our closest Friend and Intercessor with God; the
Patron of all who work, of Fathers, Husbands and Youth; the
Model of all virtues, the Guardian of Chastity, the Guide to
all who seek God in an interior life of prayer and sacrifice.

In his Apostolic Letter *'At the Beginning of the New
Millennium'*, January 2001, Pope John Paul hoped that
the Great Jubilee's legacy for the world would be an
increase in holiness. At the same time, the World of
Work Committee of the Bishops' Conference of England
and Wales published *'A Spirituality of Work'*, calling
attention to the 'Gospel of Work' which teaches that life
is not compartmentalised, and that the necessity of work
is a means to the holiness for which every man and
woman is created. Thoughts turn naturally to Saint
Joseph, their universal patron.

This heroic figure emerges from the Gospel's Infancy Narratives as an influential model for all who aspire to do God's will through the faithful accomplishment of daily tasks. St Matthew (1:19) calls him *'vir justus'*, a 'righteous' man, who possesses the gifts of the Spirit in abundance. (cf. *Is* 11:2-3). *'Iaddiq'*, the equivalent Hebrew adjective, describes honourable fidelity to the terms of any agreement and its responsibilities. Joseph was righteous in that he understood what was expected of him in the Covenant, and was determined to conform his own will to that of the Lord. In his case this was to be the foster-father of God's Son and the husband of His Virgin Mother.

The current restoration of Saint Joseph's Chapel in Westminster Cathedral inspires a surge of confidence in the Guardian of the Redeemer. Today, he remains the exemplar of persevering honesty, the incomparable pattern for fathers of families, and now cares for all God's children as they undertake their responsibilities in the world. The foster-father from whom the Carpenter of Nazareth Himself was happy to learn, is now supremely placed to support all who work for justice, peace, and well-being, within and between families and nations, for the glory of God and their own sanctification.

J. B. Midgley,
Downham Market,
Advent, 2002.

COMPANION TO SAINT JOSEPH

by
J. B. Midgley

All booklets are published thanks to the
generous support of the members of the
Catholic Truth Society

CATHOLIC TRUTH SOCIETY
PUBLISHERS TO THE HOLY SEE

CONTENTS

All rights reserved. First published 2002 by The Incorporated Catholic Truth Society 40-46 Harleyford Road London SE11 5AY Tel: 020 7640 0042 Fax: 020 7640 0046. Copyright © 2002 The Incorporated Catholic Truth Society.

ISBN 978 1 86082 172 1

DEVOTION TO SAINT JOSEPH

History

The Fathers of the Church and early Christians were quick to appreciate Joseph's sanctity, and acclaim his love for God and his neighbour. By the end of the third century, the Coptic Church was celebrating the Feast of 'Joseph the Carpenter' on 20th July, and a splendid altar had been dedicated to him in the Byzantine basilica built by St Helena. Because the infant Church understandably tended to focus attention on the martyrs, wider liturgical recognition was gradual. Devotion was stimulated, however, by the Greek document, *'The History of Joseph the Carpenter'*, and by the monastics who dwelt in the caves of Mount Carmel and sought holiness in lives of prayer and labour. The title of *'Nutritor Domini'* (The one who nurtures the Lord), which was accorded to Joseph, appeared in Western Martyrologies like those of Oengus and Tallach in Ireland, and the beginning of the twelfth century saw his feast being celebrated in Winchester and Ely, and a church dedicated to him in Bologna. The enthusiasm of St Bernard and St Thomas Aquinas was influential in securing an honoured place for Joseph in Christian hearts and, by the close of the fourteenth century, his feast had entered the calendars of the Franciscans, the Dominicans, and many European dioceses. The preaching of St Vincent Ferrer and St Bernardine of Siena carried local devotion farther afield, and the efforts of all these early champions were rewarded when Pope Sixtus IV (d.1484) established Joseph's Feast in the Roman Calendar on March 19th.

Pope Paul III, remembered for convening the Council of Trent and commissioning Michelangelo to paint 'The Last Judgement', endorsed the reforming zeal of the Jesuits, and the devotion to Saint Joseph which their founder, St Ignatius of Loyola, promoted. In 1623, Pope Gregory XV, who initiated secret ballots for papal elections, established the Congregation for the Propagation of the Faith, and canonised Teresa of Avila and Ignatius of Loyola, responded to requests of the Emperor Ferdinand and King Charles II of Spain, by making the Feast of 19th March a Holy Day of Obligation. In 1714, Pope Clement XI composed the liturgical Office still in use, but the day is no longer one when the faithful are required to hear Mass.

St John Baptist de la Salle (1651-1719), Patron of all Teachers, is another shining example of love for the Saint under whose special protection and patronage he placed his Institute. He encouraged his Brothers of the Christian Schools to acquire a reputation for their devotion, composed a 'Litany of Saint Joseph' based on the Scriptures, and directed that it should be recited daily "in honour of the guardian of the Child Jesus, the spouse of His Virgin Mother, and the model of obedience to Divine Providence, love for Jesus and Mary, and angelic purity." (cf. *'The Mind and Heart of St John Baptist de la Salle'*, Edwin Bannon FSC, La-Sallia Oxford, 1999).

Devotion to Saint Joseph

The nineteenth century witnessed a universal growth in devotion to Saint Joseph, especially on the part of workers who were often exploited and impoverished. In 1847, Pope Pius IX, in an early act of his pontificate, extended to the universal Church the Feast of 'The Patronage of Saint Joseph' to be celebrated on the third Wednesday after Easter. In 1861, he approved the establishment, in Beauvais, of the Archconfraternity of Saint Joseph which welcomed the affiliation of Associates throughout France. Its aims were to extend devotion to Saint Joseph, ask his protection for the Holy Father, the Church, the well-being of Christian family life, and his intercession for the grace of a holy death. Political and economic change in the second half of the century, with attendant civil and religious controversy, brought the Church increased pastoral responsibility which was met with a series of papal and episcopal pronouncements. (See *"Reflection"*, p.74 St Joseph the Worker). During the First Vatican Council, on 8th December 1870 the Feast of the Immaculate Conception, this longest reigning pope in history enlisted Saint Joseph's powerful assistance by declaring him Patron of the Universal Church. Two of his successors, Leo XIII and St Pius X, respectively decreed that the Office of the Feast could be used in a Votive Mass on Wednesdays, and attached an indulgence of five years to the recitation of the Litany. Over the years, Joseph has been adopted as patron of nuns, carpenters, workers in general, husbands, fathers of families, and of a happy death. A vast number of churches have been dedicated to him and, in the United States, more than to any other saint.

In 1955 Pope Pius XII established the Feast of Saint Joseph the Worker to encourage workers of the world to rely on him as their Patron whose fidelity to daily tasks exemplifies that, with God's grace, holiness is attained by embracing the duties and responsibilities of the state of life to which one is called. The new Feast on May 1st replaced that of the Patronage, previously celebrated on the third Wednesday after Easter, the date being selected to counterbalance the Communist associations of May Day. On 19th March, 1961, Pope John XXIII entrusted the deliberations of the Second Vatican Council to Saint Joseph's guidance, and ordained that his altar in St Peter's should be embellished to befit a special and efficacious Christian devotion. On November 13th, the second day of the Council, he inserted Joseph's name after Mary's, and before all the Apostles, popes, and martyrs, in the Roman

Canon of the Mass. In 2013 his name was added to the other three Eucharistic Prayers. This ensured that his eminent role in the eternal plan of salvation, love for God and neighbour, and unhesitating obedience to the Divine will in the most demanding circumstances, would always be remembered in the Sacrifice of Redemption.

In 1989, Pope John Paul II wrote his Apostolic Exhortation *'Redemptoris Custos'* (Guardian of the Redeemer) which guides the structure of these pages, and to which specific reference is made. He reminds the world that the Fathers of the Church, inspired by the Gospel, explain that just as Joseph took loving care of Mary and dedicated himself to Jesus' upbringing, now he watches over His Mystical Body and its members. The Pope says the time has come for renewed devotion to the Patron of the universal Church, and a more ardent love for the Saviour whom he fostered in such an exemplary manner. "By reflecting upon the way in which Mary's spouse shared in the divine mystery, the Church, with all humanity on the road to the future, will discover anew her own identity within the redemptive plan founded upon the mystery of the Incarnation. In this Joseph shared like no other being except Mary, the Mother of the Incarnate Word…he was involved in the same salvific event; he was the guardian of the same love, through the power of which the eternal Father 'destined us to be His children through Jesus Christ' (*Ep* 1:5)" (*'Guardian of the Redeemer'* 1).

Images of Joseph

It was not until the middle of the fourth century, that the Church finally endorsed the writings and structure of New Testament, and separated them from the apocryphal documents based on an oral tradition which, with the Old Testament and reason, had supported doctrine and devotion. The 'Infancy Gospel of James', for example, tells how Joachim and Anne, the parents of Mary, presented her in the Temple when she was three years old, an early dedication to God's will which the Church celebrates in the feast of 21st November.

When she was twelve, the High Priest began the search for a righteous man to be her husband by calling all the men of the tribe of Judah to come to the Temple with their staves. Joseph was chosen when his "rod of Jesse", the "mystic branch" of the Messiah's family tree, miraculously blossomed and a dove alighted on his head.

To counter aspersions cast by opponents of Christianity, the apocrypha defended the virginal character of the Mother of God by presenting Joseph as an elderly widower, with grown-up children, because such a one would prove a venerable custodian of her virginity. The 'Infancy Gospel of Thomas' even has him finding it difficult to cope with his precocious Foster-Son! Such an image may account for the rather comical ancient of mediaeval Mystery Plays, and the verse in the legendary 'Cherry Tree Carol', "Joseph was an old man, an old man was he when he wedded Mary in the land of Galilee." Other doubters of Mary's virginity suggested that she and Joseph had children after Jesus, their opinion based on the Gospel reference to "the brothers and sisters of the Lord" (e.g. *Mt* 13:55-56). This is but a Semitic designation of "kinsfolk" or "clan", and accords with the teaching of the Fathers and the Church regarding Mary's perpetual virginity, and Joseph's own voluntary chastity. Certainly, he was young and vigorous enough to bring his precious charges safely through acute dangers with admirable and competent fortitude. (*cf. 'Dogmatic Constitution on the Church', 'Lumen Gentium'* 64).

Joseph in Art

Familiar artistic impressions include the Nativity scenes painted by the great masters, but perhaps it is among the icons originating in the Christian East that the clearest expressions of spiritual devotion and appreciation of Joseph's eminence are to be found. Whether he is depicted as grey-bearded and elderly, or as the younger man of later opinion, the sterling dependability of his character shines through. In his right hand he usually holds a lily, the symbol of purity, with the Child Jesus is on his left arm in a pose reminiscent of the renowned depiction of 'Our Lady of Perpetual Succour.' Later, western versions soften the formality and highlight the warmth of mutual love. In another Byzantine icon, Mary watches Joseph wrestling with doubts sown by Satan, a menacing figure in an animal skin. She prays for his victory won through his unswerving faith and dedication. Sometimes a little demon hovers at his shoulder, vainly tempting human frailty so as to hinder the progress of the Incarnation. Of course, the success of God's plan was not dependent on Joseph's co-operation but, from all eternity, He knew that his response to invitation would, like Mary's, be whole-hearted. The blessed result is illustrated in an icon of the Holy Family in which the Divine Child proudly has His arms around the shoulders of both parents.

Modern versions which demonstrate a reassessment of Joseph's age, include 'St Joseph of Nazareth' by Robert Lentz, and Patricia Resmondo's 'Jubilee Icon'. In the first, the Infant Jesus lovingly embraces a dark-haired, younger Joseph on the day of His Presentation in the Temple. The Greek letters in His halo spell the divine name revealed to Moses, "I am Who am.". Also in the picture are the cave at Bethlehem, the Temple in Jerusalem, the city Jeremiah calls "throne of the Lord" (13:7), and the two doves which are the offering of the poor. In the 'Jubilee Icon', a virile Joseph teaches his twelve year old Son to catch fish which leap eagerly into the net! The scene is resonant of Jesus' familiarity with the trade, and His call to fishermen to be His Apostles. In the background, a small boat represents the Church, a reminder that all are called to be "fishers of men." On the horizon, a rising sun heralds the dawning of a new creation by the Sun of Righteousness.

Less familiar but noteworthy art includes the festive 'Betrothal of Mary and Joseph', a 16th century ceiling fresco by Pasquale Cati in the church of Santa Maria Trastavere in Rome. Then, Durer's meditative 'Flight into Egypt' sees a vulnerable, dependent, near-naked Baby in His Mother's arms, His divinity suspended as, not for the only time, a donkey provides His transport. Joseph walks beside them, his face a picture of reliable, tender solicitude, and younger than in the same artist's earlier woodcut of the Nativity. The Joseph shrine in Montreal portrays a youthful, shining example of husband and father, energetic qualities similarly evident in the Italian stained-glass 'St Joseph Worker' by Angelo Gatto, and the active craft skills of God's efficient mentor in Christopher Hobbs' ceiling mosaic in the Joseph chapel in Westminster Cathedral.

PREPARATIONS FOR THE INCARNATION

The fulfilment of God's promises

"Listen now, House of David… The Lord Himself will give you a sign… The Virgin is with child and will give birth to a son whom she will call 'Emmanuel' which means 'God is with us'… For there is a child born for us, a son given to us and dominion is laid on his shoulders… Wide is his dominion in a place which has no end, for the throne of David and for his royal power which he establishes and makes secure in justice and integrity… A root springs from the stock of Jesse, a scion thrusts from his roots." (*Is* 7:10-14; 9:7; 11:1).

In Isaiah's 'Emmanuel' prophecy, God informs the House of David that its deliverance is at hand in the person of His Son who is to assume human nature, conceived and born of a virgin mother. She is to call him 'Emmanuel', 'God is with us', a name which intimates the Messianic power to liberate God's people from oppression. To name a child was a father's prerogative but, in this case, the extraordinary virginal conception justifies departure from the norm. The House of David stands for the entire human race created by the Father, which the Son is about to join and make all men and women His brothers and sisters. The Word made Flesh comes to free them all from the powers of evil and, through His Sacrifice, to reconcile them to the Father once and for all.

St Matthew's Gospel records the "genealogy of Jesus Christ, son of David, son of Abraham…and Jacob was the father of Joseph the husband of Mary; of her was born Jesus who is called Christ." The name 'Christ', from the Greek and Aramaic 'anointed', was an epithet ascribed to the eagerly awaited King whom God promised through His prophets as the hope of salvation. The title which described this King's character most fully was 'Son of David', the salutation with which the Jews would hail Our Lord as Messiah when He entered the Holy City on Palm Sunday. He is also called 'Son of Abraham' because He fulfills God's promise to the patriarchs, "All the tribes of the earth shall bless themselves by you." Though it is clear from Isaiah's Emmanuel prophecy, and St Paul (*Rm* 1:3), that Mary herself was of the family of David, Jewish genealogical usage ignored descent from the female line, so Matthew traces Our Lord's human ancestry through Joseph, the legally registered father who validates His Davidic descent.

Nazareth, a place chosen by God

We first meet Mary and Joseph, her intended husband, in Nazareth. The place was more a village than a town, lying in the hills at the northern fringe of the Plain of

Esdraelon, some twenty miles from Tiberias, and overlooking the trade routes which linked the Jordan Valley to the Mediterranean Coast. With a population of fewer than two hundred, it did not attract a mention by Josephus, the Jewish historian, nor an inclusion in the 'Talmud', the corpus of Jewish and ceremonial law and legend. Nathanael, the future Apostle Bartholomew, dismissed it as a place from which nothing worthwhile was likely to emerge (*Jn* 1:26), but this might just be merely a sign of inter-community rivalry.

The site of a village house which Joseph would provide for his family, and with which Jesus would become familiar, was usually determined by the availability of water. This highly-prized commodity depended on cisterns for its supply, and it was a particularly fortunate location which could boast more than one well. The modest dwellings were close together, often with a vine trained to grow against one wall, and narrow alley-ways for passage and refuse disposal. We learn from Our Lord's parable about the Importunate Friend who wakes his neighbour in the middle of the night to borrow a loaf of bread (*Lk* 11:1-13), that such houses had only one room. Beds were laid out on the floor, and the irritated householder had to clamber over his wife and children to light a candle and open a creaking door. The prophecies that Jesus would be called a Nazarene are realised, (*Mt* 2:23), and the obscurity of

His home, and scene of His childhood and early manhood, is not a surprise in the light of Isaiah's prediction that the Messiah would grow up in an environment which would seem far from glorious to the eyes of the world. (*Is 53; and cf. Ps 21*). Nevertheless, it would be immortalised in Pilate's sentence of execution, "Jesus of Nazareth, King of the Jews", the superscription on the Cross, the sign of salvation and everlasting monument to Christ the King.

In his Gospel, Luke does not give biographical details about the betrothed couple or why they lived in Nazareth. He thinks it more important to celebrate the coming of the Messiah and the Kingdom he brings and, like Matthew, he draws attention to the importance of Joseph's Davidic descent as Our Lord's legal father (*Lk 1:27*). The assumption that Joseph originally came from David's royal city of Bethlehem is not proven, but there is no doubt that he was a carpenter (*cf. Mt 13:55*) who earned his living by making furniture, and the wooden components of buildings, tools, and equipment. Life was harsh, even for craftsmen who were only slightly less poor than those who sought employment in agriculture, like the labourers who queued at dawn in the market place hoping to be hired for a day's work in the landowners' vineyards. (*cf. Mt 20:1-16*). Labour supply generally exceeded demand, so the consequent competition for work kept income pitifully low. If Joseph had, indeed, moved from Bethlehem to Nazareth, it might have been because a small place needed only one carpenter who would be without competition. Though workers were often exploited, manual labour carried no stigma and was held in high regard by the rabbinical class. Rich and poor mixed socially without embarrassment, but little effort was made to alleviate dire poverty, the causes of debt, consequent extortion, and the anxiety which accompanied a precarious existence.

ANNUNCIATION AND VISITATION

When the time came for Isaiah's prophecy to come to fruition, God sent Gabriel to Mary. The Archangel greeted her, "Hail, full of grace, the Lord is with you." He told the startled girl that she was going to have a child who would be the son of the Most High God. Joachim and Anne had taught their daughter to reverence the Scriptures which she had discussed and learned them by heart in the synagogue school, but the familiarity of Isaiah's words did not prevent her mystified alarm. Since she was a virgin, how could this possibly happen? Moreover, she was betrothed to Joseph in a relationship more sacred and binding than an engagement. Gabriel explained that her baby would be conceived through the power of the Holy Spirit and, echoing Isaiah, told her to call him 'Jesus' which means 'God saves'. Then he gave her a sign that nothing was beyond God's power. Her elderly relative, Elizabeth the wife of the priest Zechariah, was now expecting their first baby in three months time, even though she had previously been infertile. In response to Gabriel's Annunciation, Mary immediately declared herself the Lord's obedient handmaiden, willing to co-operate in everything which God planned for her so that, through His Son, "the world might be saved." (*Jn* 3:16-18). Selflessly, she set off on a journey of sixty miles, not to test the truth of Gabriel's news about Elizabeth's miraculous condition, but to help her until her baby was born. (*Lk* 1:26-56).

Joseph's dilemma

When she returned to Nazareth after John the Baptist's birth, Mary's own pregnancy was obvious. Joseph must have been devastated. He knew he was not the father of the expected baby and, as yet, knew nothing of the mystery of the Incarnation which had taken place. He could have suspected Mary of infidelity, but he transcended a natural male jealousy and, despite his pain, treated his betrothed with sensitivity. Any apparent act of infidelity during the betrothal period was tantamount to adultery, and he was conscious of the Law which required an adulterous woman to be stoned to death so that the honour of the House of Israel should be preserved. Worse still, as the wronged husband, he would be called upon to cast the first stone. (*cf. Dt* 22:23). Even if a court found Mary innocent, the adverse publicity would be cruelly undeserved, for no one knew the beauty and goodness of her character as he did. He thought about completing the marriage and celebrating a conception which the betrothal period legitimised, but this raised another problem. As a devout observer of the Law, he felt that to acknowledge the child as his own, and take Mary home as his wife, was a deception contrary to his duty to God, his neighbour, and to Mary herself. Though it would shatter his dreams of life-long marriage to the girl he loved, he determined on another course of action. The Law did not oblige the injured party to denounce Mary in front of the village tribunal, so he decided on the alternative of issuing a private bill of divorce in the presence of two witnesses without seeking redress in the courts. Though Mary had been away a long time and despite knowing nothing about Gabriel's message of Annunciation, the 'just man' never doubted her innocence, and sensed there was a supernatural explanation for her pregnancy which was consistent with her virtue. Maybe he heard echoes of the Prophets and remembered how his own ancestry figured in the cherished expectations of the Messiah.

Joseph participates in God's plan

As he slept, "an Angel" visited Joseph in a dream, and we shall assume that it is always Gabriel whom God has commissioned to prepare the way for the Incarnation by co-ordinating the details of His plan. He told him to have no misgivings about taking Mary home as his wife, because it was through the power of the Holy Spirit that she had conceived. He was to call the baby 'Jesus', 'God saves', because He would save all the people from their sins. Thus, he introduced Joseph to the mystery of Mary's motherhood and constant virginity, restored his right and duty to give the baby a name, and transferred to him all the privileges and responsibilities of earthly fatherhood.

"When Joseph woke up he did what the angel of the Lord had told him to do." (*Mt* 1:24).

Joseph's courage and unquestioning faith in resigning himself to the divine will is wonderful. He did not share our advantage of being able to view the entire Gospel panorama and benefit from the comforting, collective wisdom of inspired Christian teaching, or experience God in the gentle humanity of Christ. We are supported by two millennia of belief in the doctrine of the Holy Trinity, so we are not astonished by Gabriel's explanation of Mary's motherhood, but of Joseph it required a huge leap of trust. What is more, the God whom he worshipped was 'Yhwh', a title so holy that it was pronounced only by the high priest in the Temple once a year. The alternative 'Adonai', 'Lord', was preferred so that the sacred name might not be uttered in vain. Yet here was this angel telling him to call a baby 'Yehoshua', 'Yhwh Saves' (Jesus). Many would feel inclined to stand up for their own rights with some aggression, but Joseph has the strength of the meek and humble of heart, and becomes a willing agent of God's entry into humanity.

In Old Testament times angelic visitations were received with some trepidation since they were often associated with disconcerting news, like a forecast of one's own imminent demise, but Joseph did not flinch. He emulated Mary, in accepting Gabriel's news of her motherhood and virginal conception of the Messiah without asking for an explanation. He escorted her home as his wife, completed the marriage, and welcomed her expected Baby with the readiness he invariably shows in all that God asks of him. The Law established family relationship, not by biological descent but by the recognition of legitimate parentage including that which is established by adoption. Joseph may not be a father in the biological sense but, in every other way, by consent, love, nurture and guidance, he is the true and legal father to Jesus, and his fatherhood is closest to God's own. A Saviour is born of the House and family of David to accomplish His royal and Messianic mission, and through Joseph's willingness to undertake paternal responsibility symbolised in the naming of a child, God keeps the promised He made to Abraham and David. (*cf. Mt* 1:1-24; *'Guardian of the Redeemer'* 2, 3).

THE NATIVITY

The Census

Mary's baby was due when the emperor Caesar Augustus called for a census of the population, the usual method the Romans employed to estimate the revenue which could be expected from the taxes levied. Rome took 25% of the Jews' income, and Temple taxes swallowed a further 22%, so precious little was left for a worker and his family on which to survive. Every citizen was required to register in his place of origin, so Joseph, who was of the royal House and family of David, had to travel from Nazareth to Bethlehem, the Judaean town six miles south of Jerusalem where David had been born and anointed king of Israel. Though a wife was not obliged to attend with her husband for registration, Mary wanted to be with Joseph, and took with her the swaddling clothes in which to wrap a new-born infant. The Gospel does not comment on the rigours of a sixty-mile journey in such circumstances. Clearly it demanded courage, and Joseph would have been anxious for his young bride and expectant mother, but the prophecy that the Saviour would be born in Bethlehem was to be fulfilled. "But you Bethlehem Ephrathah, the least of the clans of Judah, out of you will be born for me the one who is to rule over Israel; his origin goes back to the distant past, to the days of old." Even the Roman emperor was an unlikely servant in God's plan. (*cf. Mi* 5:1).

No sooner had they arrived in Bethlehem than Mary went into labour. To his dismay, Joseph could not find any suitable lodgings for her because of the numbers coming to register for the census. The only place available was a cave used as an animal shelter, and in these uncongenial surroundings he acted as midwife for Mary. She wrapped their Baby in the swaddling clothes and used a feeding-box as His cradle. Though she and Joseph never imagined that the long-awaited Messiah would choose to come into the world in such lowly circumstances, pain and worry gave way to unspoken joy. By going to Bethlehem for the census, Joseph obeyed legitimate, earthly authority, and officially inserted the name "Jesus, son of Joseph of Nazareth" (*Jn* 1:45) in the register of the Roman Empire. "The registration clearly shows that Jesus belongs to the human race as a man among men, a citizen of the world, subject to laws and civil institutions, but also Saviour of the world. He was born before the census was completed so, by being registered with everyone, He sanctified everyone; inscribed with the whole world in the census, he offered to the world communion with Himself and, after presenting Himself, He wrote all the people of the world in the Book of the living." ('*Guardian of the Redeemer*' 9).

The Adoration of the Shepherds

Joseph's vigilant presence is evident throughout the Infancy Narratives. He is the guardian of the mystery hidden in the mind of God before time began, and, after the birth of His Son, he is witness to the adoration of the shepherds. Judaea was sheep-rearing country, and Bethlehem a traditional and convenient centre for men who tended their masters' flocks. On the night of Jesus' birth, some of them were amazed by the sudden appearance of an angel "radiant in the Lord's own glorious light". Gabriel calmed their fears with the wonderful news of the Saviour's birth, and told them where they could find Him. He was joined by a heavenly choir praising God and announcing His peace to all people of good will. The penalties exacted for the loss or abandonment of sheep were severe, so it was with brave trust that these shepherds left their flocks and hurried down to the town where they found Mary and Joseph, with their new-born Baby wrapped in swaddling clothes and cradled in a manger, just as Gabriel had described. They repeated everything the Angel had said, and this confirmation of the Annunciation's details assured the new parents who treasured the knowledge that their Son Jesus had come into history as a man, and He was the Redeemer of the world. The shepherds returned to their flocks giving glory to God and thanking Him because they had found the Truth about whom the Angel had spoken.

Extreme poverty and a relentlessly demanding occupation, caused shepherds to live on the fringes of society, maybe even on the edge of the law. They were regarded with some suspicion, and the rabbinical class was particularly critical of a life style which seemed incompatible with an exact observance of the regulations governing religious practice. However, it was not to powerful rulers or professional religious leaders that God sent His angels to make the first announcement of Creation's most important event. While the world slept, He showed His love for humble hearts by inviting watchful shepherds to be the first visitors to His Son who, one day would describe Himself, and be forever loved, as the Good Shepherd. Mary and Joseph witness that it is to the poor, the unpretentious, and those who care for the vulnerable, that the Good News of the Kingdom is first entrusted. (*cf. Mt* 1:1-25; *Lk* 2:1-20; 7:22; *'Guardian of the Redeemer'* 10).

AFTER THE NATIVITY

The Circumcision

Adam and Eve abused the free-will with which God had dignified the human race, but, in His changeless and merciful love, He immediately promised redemption and salvation for them and all their descendants. He repeated this covenant to Noah after the deluge which had resulted from continued disobedience, and He declared that it would last until the end of time. Later, He assured Abraham that he would become the "father of a multitude of nations"…in whom all would be blessed, and his descendants would live in the land of Canaan as the favoured trustees of the Covenant. As a sign of this special agreement, God ordained that every male child should have his foreskin circumcised when he was eight days old. "My Covenant shall be marked on your bodies as a Covenant in perpetuity." (*cf. Gn* 12:1-7; 17:9-14). God demonstrates the limitless love He has for all His children, the entire humanity He creates, in His patient care for the people of Israel whom He freed from slavery in Egypt and brought them back to the specially chosen land. He gave Moses His Law on Mount Sinai to help them combat the virus of sin, asking them in return only to recognise and serve Him as the one, true, and living

God. To give them the hope of salvation planned for all nations, He would send His prophets and His own beloved Son to reveal His love and prove His fidelity in a new and eternal covenant. (*cf. Ex* 19:6ff; *Lv* 12:3).

In the former Covenant, circumcision was a sacrament of legal observance and a sign of initiation into the service of God. This celebration of a boy's admission to spiritual communion with Israel, and his share in God's promise to Abraham and the patriarchs, symbolised a contract between God and the boy who, thereupon, embraced the Law with all its privileges and responsibilities. Contrary to artistic imagination, circumcision was performed, not in the Temple but in private houses, the more public synagogue ceremony being introduced at a later date. By the time Jesus was to be circumcised, Joseph had found more suitable accommodation for his family once the initial demands for accommodation occasioned by the census had eased. He presented his Boy for this first redemptive shedding of blood, and gave Him the name 'Jesus', the significance of which he had learned from the Angel, "for He will save the people from their sins."

In exercising the right and duty to bestow "the only name in which there is salvation", Joseph claims his legal fatherhood and makes the official announcement of the Child's Messianic mission. The Saviour born to the people of Israel presents Himself as the appointed heir to the promises which His heavenly Father had made to

Abraham. This Spotless Lamb, to whom all power is given in heaven and on earth is not subject to the Law. He has no need of circumcision, but He has chosen to be born under God's Law in the world of men, and to this He teaches obedience so that all justice should be fulfilled. He comes to bring the Law to perfection, and, in His human flesh, show that He is indeed a descendant of Abraham. The Son of Man is a true son of the race chosen to bring forth the Messiah, and, in subjecting Himself to circumcision, He abides by the covenant of which the Old Testament rite is a sign. (*cf. Ac* 4:12; *Mt* 28:18; *Lk* 2:21; *'Guardian of the Redeemer'* 11, 12).

The Presentation in the Temple

"The Lord spoke to Moses, 'Consecrate all the first-born to me, the first issue of among the sons of Israel... If a woman conceives and gives birth to a boy, she is to be unclean for seven days. On the eigth day the child's foreskin must be circumcised, and she must wait another thirty-three days for her blood to be purified... Then she is to bring to the priest...a lamb, one year old, for a holocaust, and a young pigeon or turtle-dove as a sacrifice for sin. If she cannot offer a lamb, one year old, she is to take two turtle-doves or two young pigeons, one for the holocaust, and the other as a sacrifice for sin. The priest is to perform the rite of atonement over her and she will be purified." (*Ex* 13:2; *Lv* 12:2-8).

Joseph took his family to the Temple for his wife's purification, and to meet his fatherly obligation to present Jesus to God and "redeem" Him (*cf. Nb* 18:15) with the offering of the poor, a pair of turtle-doves, or two young pigeons. Though the Saviour came to Israel as God's delegate and anointed heir to the promises He made through His prophets, His first visit to the Temple was not marked by any great ceremonial pomp. Nothing distinguished the Holy Family from the other worshippers present, but the prophecies came true, and the the rituals confirmed that the Lord is one with His people in their humanity. The First-born of all creation represents the people of the Covenant who, ransomed from slavery, now belong to God once more. As the author of Redemption, Jesus is not the one to be redeemed. He is the true price of ransom who satisfies and transcends the Old Testament ritual requirements, but again He submits Himself to the Law for our edification. At His Presentation, doves are offered but, on His last day in Jerusalem, He Himself will be the sacrifice. (*cf. 'Guardian of the Redeemer'* 13).

Appropriately, Our Lord was greeted by Simeon, a pious Levite priest who observed the Law with a worthy shepherd's zeal. He had been inspired to visit the Temple that day, and was keeping prayerful watch with Anna, a devout, elderly prophetess. To the world, they might not seem very important, yet they are chosen to welcome the Messiah and shed light upon

His future about which Joseph and Mary were still unaware. A life-time of prayer gave Simeon wisdom to understand the promptings of the Holy Spirit, and recognise the Child as the hoped-for Messiah who would restore Israel's fortunes and bring the light of revelation to all the nations. Having made this announcement according to God's will, he said he was content to depart this life in peace, but warned that Jesus' mission would not be a populist triumph. His message would test the sincerity of people's innermost thoughts, and some would respond only with opposition and contempt, but no one would remain unaffected, even those who refused to accept Him. Simeon's final prediction that a sword of sorrow would pierce Mary's heart did not leave Joseph untouched, but Anna offers consolation. She praised and thanked God for the arrival of the Child to all who eagerly awaited the deliverance of Jerusalem and the liberation of Sion from Satan's malign influence. Like the shepherds, and the Magi already on their way, Simeon and Anna represent everyone welcome in God's Kingdom without distinction, and they show that faith and a receptive spirit are more important than status in becoming aware of Christ. Joseph took his family home, amazed at their reception in the Temple, and he and Mary were left with much to think about. (cf. Mt 1:1-25; Lk 2:21-28; 'Guardian of the Redeemer' 13)

The Coming of the Magi: a revelation to the Nations

Herod the Great still ruled with savage self-interest in Judaea when three wise men from the East arrived in Jerusalem and enquired where they might find the new-born king of the Jews. They had discovered a star, the sign of a ruler, in the East, which had guided them on their long journey to pay him the homage. 'Magi' (Greek 'Magor') were wise persons who interpreted dreams, or astrologers who calculated the significance of signs in the heavens. The word has nothing to do with magicians, the tricksters who tried witchcraft to summon mosquitoes, or the sorcerer Simon Magus. (*Ex 8:12; Ac* 8:9ff). The three who came to see Our Lord were probably from Arabia, Mesopotamia or Babylon, and are first identified as kings by Tertullian (d 225) who based his supposition on Isaiah's prophecy and David's Psalm: "The nations come to your bright light and kings to your dawning brightness…the wealth of the nations comes to you; everyone in Sheba will come bringing gold and incense, and singing the praise of the Lord… The kings of Tarshish and the sea coasts shall pay him tribute, The kings of Sheba and Seba shall bring him gold." (*Is* 10:6; *Ps* 71). Sheba was a town inherited by another Simeon, a leader of one of Israel's twelve tribes, and Seba was another in South West Arabia. The names which tradition gives to the Magi are Caspar, Melchior and Balthasar, and they are especially venerated in Cologne Cathedral where there relics are said to repose.

Herod and his subjects were taken aback by the Magi's arrival and request for directions to a new king. When the throne's current occupant consulted the chief priests and scribes, he found little comfort in their confirmation that a leader would be born in Bethlehem who would be a "true Shepherd" to the kingdom of Israel, a title associated with royal authority and responsibility nobly undertaken. (*Mi* 5:1). Herod asked his visitors to go to Bethlehem, find the Child, and call on their way back to tell him where exactly he could pay his own respects. As soon as the Magi left him, the star reappeared and guided them to where Jesus lay, and they were overjoyed to worship Him. Though memories of the Scriptures must have stirred in Joseph's mind, he wondered at these impressive strangers who acknowledged his Child as the Son of God with their gifts. They brought gold for a King whose realm is of justice and peace, the frankincense of sacrifice for a Priest who sanctifies the people and restores them to the Father, and bitter myrrh for the Victim who immolates Himself on the altar of the Cross to draw all things to Himself. Before the Magi left Bethlehem, Gabriel advised them, as they slept, to avoid Herod by circumventing Jerusalem on their return journey. (*Mt* 2:1-12 and *cf. 'Guardian of the Redeemer'* 10).

The Escape to Egypt

No sooner had the Magi set off on their journey home than Gabriel came to Joseph in a dream and told him to take his family to Egypt because Herod was determined to kill Jesus whom he saw as a rival for his throne. An urgency of tone indicated that delay would be fatal, so, without asking for details or assistance, Joseph left with Mary and the Baby that same night. He must have been sick with fear on their behalf as he hastily organised their departure, hiding his own anxiety while anticipating the horrors of a six-day journey to reach Egypt's frontiers. This country was now a prefecture of the Roman Empire and, with a Jewish population of about a million, had become a traditional and relatively convenient sanctuary from any oppression encountered in Israel. Joseph protected Jesus and Mary from persecution at home and sought asylum abroad, but no welfare or social services were accessible, and he had to support them by casual work. No doubt he was exploited but, as always in the Scripture story, his silence is an eloquent acceptance of his awesome responsibilities. (*cf. 'Guardian of the Redeemer'* 14).

From earliest times, the Feast of the Epiphany has been associated with the Nativity Of Our Lord, and the Church continues to celebrate His revelation to the Gentile world, personified by the Magi, twelve days after Christmas. However, their visit must have taken place after the Presentation perhaps by as much as a year. St Matthew says the wise men entered "the house", which indicates that Joseph had found more permanent accommodation after the Census. It was more convenient

to stay near Jerusalem for the Circumcision and
Presentation than to travel back and forth to Nazareth,
and maybe he had decided to make Bethlehem his home
again. The Magi's visit, the aftermath of the Gabriel's
warning and the escape to Egypt, could not have
preceded the Presentation which would have involved a
highly dangerous visit to the Temple in the city, where
Herod held court. The king was furious when he realised
the Magi had eluded him and ordered the military to
slaughter every male child, under two years of age, in
Bethlehem and its vicinity. The sacrifice of innocent
children to safeguard his own position meant nothing to
him, but it intensified the fears of Mary and Joseph when
the news filtered through. The fact that Herod callously
allowed a two-year margin of error in the Massacre of the
Innocents adds weight to the supposition that the Magi's
visit took place a considerable time after the Presentation
when Jesus would have been only six weeks old.

It is natural that St Matthew, a Jew writing principally
for Jewish converts to Christianity, should draw attention
to Our Lord's Messianic Kingship. He is the only
Evangelist to tell the Magi story with its warning that
human nature can react badly when power and self-
interest are challenged, and the slaughter of the innocent
children brings the account of the wise men's visit to a
sad conclusion. Matthew's audience would have
remembered, with Mary and Joseph, how Pharaoh had

hunted the infant Moses born, like Jesus, to bring freedom to captives. It is a sad irony that the ruler of the Chosen People tries to kill their Messiah, while Gentile foreigners, worship Him with their gifts. Balaam, a pagan soothsayer and forerunner of the Magi, was ordered by Balek, king of the Moabites, to curse the Israelites but was inspired by God to bless them instead. "A star from Jacob takes the leadership, and a sceptre arises from Israel." (*Nb* 24:17). The wisdom and faith of the Magi enabled them to see in a helpless baby the Star who unites divinity with humanity, and time with eternity.

From Egypt to Nazareth

Within the year, in April near the Feast of Passover, Herod died from a previously contracted illness, though at the time of the Magi's visit there was no sign that it would prove fatal. His elder son Archelaus, whom he had nominated to succeed him, was duly acclaimed king of Judaea-Samaria, but Augustus Caesar kept him waiting six months for imperial confirmation, and then granted him the title only of Ethnarch or provincial governor. Joseph was asleep when Gabriel told him of Herod's death and that, with that danger removed, he could take Jesus and Mary back to Israel. The words of the prophet Hosea, "When Israel was a child I loved him, and I called my son out of Egypt" (11:1), are evocative of Israel's exile, the providential rehearsal for Christ's own return to save the scattered sheep of Israel, and God's fidelity to His promises throughout all ages.

It was with a lighter heart that Joseph journeyed homeward with his family, no doubt intending to return to Bethlehem, if not to live there at least to put his affairs in order. It was while on the Egypt-Gaza-Azotus road that he first heard about the succession of Archelaus. The new ruler had also inherited his father's unsavoury reputation, so Judaea was still a dangerous place for Jesus who had already been targeted as a pretender for the throne. After a further dream-warning had confirmed his fears, Joseph turned his steps towards Galilee where the less menacing Antipas was ruler, and settled again in Nazareth where he and Mary had lived and married. Jesus has adopted the mantle of Moses and, like Israel's great law-giver, has now spent time in Egypt, crossed desert and water, and brings to a new Israel His teaching which will begin on another mountain. (*cf. Mt* 5). "Just as Israel had followed the path of the exodus from 'the condition of slavery' in Egypt in order to begin the Old Covenant, so Joseph, guardian and co-operator in the providential mystery of God, even in exile watched over the One who brings about the New Covenant." (*'Guardian of the Redeemer'* 14; *cf. Mt* 2:1-23).

THE FINDING IN THE TEMPLE

Every year in March or April, the Jews celebrated the Feast of Passover to commemorate the escape of the Israelites from Egypt. It was also called the Feast of Unleavened Bread in remembrance of the meal which God had told their ancestors to prepare and eat hastily before their Exodus. From all over the Roman world, pilgrims went to Jerusalem to celebrate the Feast in the holy city and the Temple. At the age of twelve, a Jewish boy became a "son of the Law" and responsible for observing its obligations so, a few months after Jesus' twelfth birthday, Joseph and Mary took Him to the city for His first visit since His Presentation in the Temple as a baby. The conscious experience of being in His Father's house was to be of profound significance. After the Passover celebration, Joseph and Mary began the return journey to Nazareth but were unaware that Jesus had stayed in Jerusalem. This might seem careless on their part, but in the village groups which made the pilgrimage, men and women usually travelled separately, so either parent could innocently assume that a child was safely in the care of the other. Then, in Galilean society, boys of twelve exercised a degree of independence with which the West is unfamiliar. An outcome of the prevailing poverty was that children as young as this were considered mature enough to leave home and fend for themselves. If a boy was fortunate, he would be introduced to a trade by his father or another relative; if not, he dropped into the great pool of unemployed. Only when Mary and Joseph stopped for the night after a day's walk, did the awful truth dawn on them that Jesus was missing. Sick with worry they rushed back to the city and searched frantically for three long days before they found Him in the Temple, sitting with the teachers and asking them questions. Everyone there was amazed at His understanding and the answers He gave when questions were debated.

Despite the overwhelming relief at finding Jesus safe and sound, Joseph might well have taken his young charge to task for what seemed like inconsiderate behaviour. Mother Mary gently intervened, "Son, why have you treated us like this; your father and I have been worried out of our minds looking for you." They were bemused by His reply, "Why were you looking for me when, surely, you must have known that I had to attend to my Father's business." This must have been particularly painful for Joseph to whom Mary had just referred as "your father", but maybe his mind went back twelve years when the Angel told him not to be afraid to take Mary home as his wife because she had conceived the Child through the power of the Holy Spirit. "From that time on, he had known he was the guardian of the mystery of God, and it was this which Jesus brought to mind." (*'Guardian of the Redeemer'* 15).

Jesus' answer was also a reminder that as soon as a Jewish boy was twelve, he moved from the aegis of his

mother's care to his father's in order to learn his trade or
"business". In His first recorded words, the Incarnate
Word announces an absolute commitment to His Father's
plan of salvation for all mankind. His stay in the city and
its explanation to His parents are more comprehensible in
the context of His first visit to Jerusalem for His
Presentation. Then, Simeon and Anna spoke for Him
about His identity and mission, but now He is able to say
for Himself that God's claims take precedence over all
other considerations, even family relationships. Simeon's
prophecy that a sword of sorrow should pierce Mary's
heart, first experienced in the flight to Egypt, continues.
The day would come when, on a final visit to the city
with His mother and disciples to celebrate the Passover,
the Son of God would disclose His relationship with His
Heavenly Father (*cf. Jn* 14ff) and, again, be lost to them
for three days before His Resurrection. Joseph's heart
was not immune to his wife's sword of sorrow and he
must often have wondered what to do for the best. He
does not say a word, but continues to undertake his
responsibility for Jesus with sublime faith and self-denial.
He would, however, unlike his wife be spared the
fearsome pain of witnessing the Passion and Crucifixion
of the boy he called "Son". (*cf. Lk* 2:41-50)

THE HIDDEN LIFE

After His extended visit to the Temple, Jesus goes home to Nazareth and will not mention His heavenly Father again until He begins His public ministry. He was obedient to Mary and Joseph who preserved in their hearts the memory and implication of their momentous experiences. A veil descends on His early years but Luke, like the good doctor he is, records that He grew to physical maturity, advanced in wisdom with God's blessing, and won golden opinions from all with whom He came in contact. (*Lk* 2:39-40; 51-52). Jesus' humanity was no pretence and He progressed through the normal stages of development. All children are consummate imitators, and the Divine Child did not exclude Himself from the influence of His parents, especially his father, whose experiences, qualities and example became reflected in His personality. "The growth of Jesus in wisdom and in stature, and in favour with God and man took place within the Holy Family under the patriarchal eyes of Joseph who had the significant task of raising Jesus, that is, feeding, clothing, and educating Him in the Law and in a trade, in keeping with the duties of a father…The Church venerates St Joseph because He fed Him whom the faithful must eat as the Bread of eternal life." (*'Guardian of the Redeemer'* 16)

In Joseph Our Lord experiences human fatherhood, and envisages the face of His Eternal Father. He encourages us to call God "Abba", a child's intimate and confident cry of "Daddy!" which His baby lips relished in Mary's arms as she pointed to Joseph, and now echoes His filial relationship with the first Person of the Blessed Trinity. St Francis de Sales meditates upon Jesus in the arms of Joseph, experiencing the fatherly love of which His heavenly Father is the source. "What sweet kisses he received from Him, how pleasant to hear Him, as a tiny child, call him "father", and with what bliss he felt His tender embraces. An unconditional and transforming love disposed him towards Jesus as to a most gentle son given to him by the Holy Spirit through the Blessed Virgin, his wife." Years later, on a hill near the Sea of Galilee where Jesus preached His first Sermon, He eulogised the meek, the poor in spirit, those who yearn for righteousness, and the pure in heart. He must have remembered the two people who received Him with courageous and unquestioning love, clothed His nakedness, quenched His thirst, and demonstrated all the qualities which He emulated in His own human person.

Like all mothers, Mary undertook Our Lord's early education, inculcated personal, social and domestic habits directly and by example, and trained Him in the accompanying skills and practices. Both parents loved the Law and the Scriptures, and taught their Son to say His prayers, using the Psalms with which Mary's

'Magnificat' reveals detailed familiarity. (*cf. Lk* 1:46-55). Under Joseph's tutelage, He who fashioned the Universe learned carpentry, so that He might follow in His earthly father's footsteps, earn a living, and contribute to the family income by the work of His hands. Fortuitously, Isaiah has provided a description of the Redeemer's Guardian, "who has directed the Lord as His counsellor, instructed Him in the path of justice and knowledge, and showed him the way of understanding." (*Is* 40:10-1)

Jesus reciprocated the caring love of Mary and Joseph by obeying them and, in so doing, sanctified the duties of family life, and the routine obligations of work which He carried out at the side of the man He called father. When Philip told his friend Nathanael that they had found the one of whom Moses and the prophets had written, he identified the Messiah as "the son of Joseph from Nazareth". Other than Mary, no one has a more glorious title and it is right that, after her, Joseph should be revered as our most powerful advocate worthy of admiration, gratitude and devotion. On earth, he fostered the Eternal Word who made all things and, in his tender care of Jesus, he mirrors God the Father's love for all His children. Even in Nazareth, life for the Holy Family would not have been without its anxieties, for the character of Herod Antipas did not exactly inspire confidence. One day he would be responsible for the murder of Jesus' cousin, John the Baptist, and later be in Jerusalem at the time of His own betrayal and arrest. He would treat Jesus with ridicule before returning Him to Pontius Pilate for a travesty of judgement. Whatever danger, hardship, or humiliation came his way, Joseph never wavered. Every vicissitude was faced with a determination which God had seen from all eternity in His plan for humanity's happiness. (*Lk 3:28; 4:22; Jn* 1:45; 6:42).

The House at Nazareth

In 1106, a Russian monk called Abbot Daniel braved the hostile attention of the Saracens and made the dangerous journey to the Holy Land. He left a description of the Holy House at Nazareth to which Joseph brought his family on their return from Egypt. This had been incorporated into the crypt of the Church of the Annunciation where "a small cavern with two small doors gives entrance to the grotto. On the right is the dwelling where the Holy Virgin lived with her Son, Jesus, whom she raised and whose bed may still be seen. Here, too, is the sepulchre of Saint Joseph." There is a tradition that, in 1291, the House in Nazareth was miraculously brought by angels to Loreto on Italy's Adriatic coast. The dwelling, of only four hundred square feet, is enshrined in a Basilica which has attracted countless pilgrims, among them Pope John XXIII (d.1963). Until the post-Conciliar review of the Liturgy in 1970, the Feast of the Holy House of Loreto had its place in the Calendar on 10th

December, and the town's name is always remembered in the title of Our Lady's 'Litany of Loreto'. Though the brickwork and style of the house is indisputably Palestinian, some have questioned the historical veracity of its marvellous translocation. Others believe that it was an Italian family called 'de Angelis', and not our heavenly companions, who arranged for its transfer to Loreto. What remains certain throughout the ages, is that pilgrims, with penitent hearts open to God's grace, find reconciliation and solace in those places which He allows faith to sanctify.

Joseph's Legacy

Joseph's death

Joseph has withdrawn from the Gospel story by the time his foster-son is thirty and about to begin His public mission at the wedding-feast in Cana. The time has come for Jesus to speak of His heavenly Father as the centre of His mission, and there must be no ambiguity to confuse His listeners. It appears that, with his task complete, Joseph had died peacefully in the presence of Jesus and Mary, but recently enough to be remembered as Jesus' father. (*cf. Jn* 6:42). An 18th century painting of the 'Death of Joseph' by Carlo Rambaldi, inspired by *'The History of Joseph the Carpenter'*, portrays the comforting presence of Jesus and Mary, a blessing for which everyone prays in the Hymn for Morning Prayer on 19th March: "Saint of the dying, blest with Mary's presence, in death you rested in the arms of Jesus; so at our ending, Jesus, Mary, Joseph, come to assist us." In His last moments upon the Cross, Jesus remembered that widows in first century Palestine faced a bleak future, so He entrusted His mother to the care of St John, something He would not have done had His foster-father still been alive. Mary became the trustee of her Son's Church until Pentecost and, in St John's person, accepted every human being as her own child, everyone a brother and sister to her Son, and so a foster-child of her husband. (*cf Jn* 18:25-27). An American nun has written a touching poem about Our Lord's descent into Limbo to release the souls of the just who had died before Him. St Joseph is the first to greet Him: "Hello Son! How's your Mother?"

In his Scripture Commentary, St Bede the Venerable writes that Joseph's body was eventually entombed in the Valley of Josaphat, one of his Davidic ancestors through whom his foster-son inherited the Messianic throne. The spot is part of the Cedron Valley east of Jerusalem, and reputed to be the site of the Last Judgement. It seems splendidly appropriate that if this is the place where Our Lord will return in triumphant glory at the end of time, His foster-father's body should be the first to be re-united with his noble soul. (*cf. Mt* 25:31).

St Teresa of Avila (1515-82) dedicated the Mother House of her reformed Carmelite communities to the Saint, and recommended complete confidence in one whom she found always granted every favour she requested. "It seems that God has given to other saints the power to help us with particular problems, but I know from experience that Joseph helps us in all our needs. Our Lord wants us to know that just as He was obedient to His foster-father in all things here on earth, so now He still grants everything he desires in heaven." This influence is vividly illustrated in the Menorcan cathedral in Ciudadella where the Joseph Chapel has two sets of life-size statues. In the lower pair, Joseph holds Jesus' hand in the unique relationship which makes him such a powerful advocate and, above, the Divine Child in glory is still hand in hand with His haloed foster-father. The Carmelites adopted Joseph as their Patron, and, in 1689, were given permission to celebrate the Feast of his Patronage, a privilege later extended to Spain and other countries who sought the approval of the Holy See. Meanwhile, Jean Gerson, French theologian and chancellor of the University of Paris had composed a liturgical office for a feast called the 'Espousals of Mary and Joseph', and this was so warmly received by the faithful that Pope Paul III (d.1549) sanctioned its celebration on 23rd January, first to the Franciscans, and then to other religious congregations and dioceses. As 'The Betrothal of Our Lady to Saint Joseph', it had a place in the Roman Calendar until its revision after the Second Vatican Council.

Patron of a Happy Death

Saint Teresa recommended confidence in this most influential of intercessors because, just as Our Lord obeyed His foster-father on earth, so now He remains anxious to please him in Heaven. This is of particular comfort to mortals when they contemplate departure from this life and naturally recoil from a great leap into the unknown. Joseph's legacy includes the recollection of his most blessed death in the arms of Jesus and Mary and, as we move from time to eternity, he is there to ease our passage with the reassurance of their same loving presence keeping at bay the doubts of the evil one.

Patron of Homeseekers

Having moved to Nazareth, presumably from Bethlehem, Joseph met and was betrothed to Mary but was then confronted with the startling news of the Annunciation with all its painful implications. When the Census was called, he had to undertake an arduous journey back to Bethlehem where he could find nothing but a cave in which to shelter his wife who was about to give birth. Then he had to seek asylum for his family in Egypt to escape Herod's murderous threat to his foster-son. When Herod died, the character of his successor precluded a return to Judaea, so he took his family back to Nazareth. Those who seek refuge from persecution, who are worried about accommodation, finding a deposit, raising a mortgage, buying and selling a house with the associated horrors, can turn to Joseph for his sympathetic and eager assistance.

The Model of Workers

In the pure delight of the Garden of Eden, humanity lived in blissful harmony with God who wanted His Creation to share His indescribable happiness. There was no arduous, monotonous toil to keep body and soul together until Adam and Eve succumbed to Satan's envious mischief. Their disobedience let loose the virus of sin with its punishments, one of which came in the shape of unwelcome labour. "Accursed be the soil because of you," God told them. "With suffering shall you get your food from it every day of your life... With sweat on your brow shall you eat your bread." But God's mercy is immediate, and He soothes the pain with a promise of victory over the forces of evil. In the first "glad tidings" of His constant love for humanity, despite its fall from grace, He told Satan that He was putting enmity between him and the woman, between the powers of darkness and her descendants, one of whom would finally obliterate him. (*cf. Gn* 3:15;17). Thus it is that economic activity, exercised in the moral order and compatible with social justice, is enshrined in God's plan of salvation. The work of human beings, created in His image, becomes an individual and communal participation in His work of Creation, and work an honourable use of the talents and resources He has given to us. The undertaking of its demands unites us to Our Lord, the Carpenter who learned His craft from Joseph who collaborated with Him in His work of Redemption. The disciple takes up the cross of daily work which becomes a means to holiness, and things which seem mundane, or "work-a-day", become imbued with the spirit of Christ. (*cf. 'Catechism of the Catholic Church'*, 2426-7).

Pope John Paul II describes the Holy Family of Nazareth as "the model for human families in the order of salvation and holiness", and their work as a daily expression of love. "With the humanity of the Son of God, work has been embraced in the mystery of the Incarnation, and has also been redeemed in a special way… At the work-bench where he plied his trade with Jesus, Joseph brought human work closer to the mystery of Redemption. When the human personality of Jesus developed in wisdom, age and grace, the virtue of industry played a significant role, because work is a human good which transforms nature and makes man, in a sense, more human." The Pope concludes that "what is important is the sanctification of daily life which each person acquires according to his state, and this can be promoted according to a model accessible to all people. Saint Joseph is the model of those humble ones that Christianity raises to great destinies…He proves that to be a good and genuine follower of Christ, there is no need of great things. It is enough to have the common, simple and human virtues, as long as they are true and authentic." ('Guardian of the Redeemer' 22-27).

Exemplar of the Interior Life

It was in his vibrant relationship with God, fidelity to prayer and profound reverence for His word in the Scriptures, that Joseph found the strength and courage to surrender his own hopes and interests in the cause of the divine plan. Four times he received striking messages in dreams and, each time, he unhesitatingly complied with God's wishes, and accepted total responsibility for the Holy Family while nobly denying himself the natural solace of conjugal love. He was in constant contact with the Saviour who chose to live under his roof and, in this unique relationship, the exchange of fatherly and filial love enabled great decisions to be taken. It illuminates the mystery of the Incarnation, and the human nature of Our Lord which sanctifies all His brothers and sisters with a share in His divinity. "By virtue of His divinity, Christ's human actions were salvific for us, causing grace within us by merit and efficacy." (*Thomas Aquinas, 'Summa Theologica', 2-2*). The mystery of grace, the saving acts of love, are present in the Nativity, the Circumcision, the Presentation, the escape to Egypt, and the hidden life in Nazareth. Through Jesus' humanity His love shines on all, but first it shone on Mary and Joseph. (*cf. 'Guardian of the Redeemer'* 25-27).

THE LITURGY OF SAINT JOSEPH

Prayers and Litany

"Glorious Saint Joseph, whom God chose to be the foster-father of the Word Made Flesh, the comforter of His Most Holy Mother, and the faithful co-operator among men in his great design, obtain for us to do in all things the will of the Father, to cherish in our hearts the mysteries accomplished in the person of the Son and, by the abundant graces of the Holy Spirit, to serve God with a pure heart and a chaste body." (*La Sallian Prayer*).

A Novena to Saint Joseph

Glorious Saint Joseph, God entrusted the Infant Jesus and His Mother, the Virgin of Virgins, to your faithful care. Through your holy intercession with your foster-son, may we stay free from sin and serve Jesus and Mary all the days of our life. Guide and protect the Holy Church and our Holy Father the Pope, and pray for us who have recourse to you so that, after this present life, we may all come to the glory in Heaven which you obtain for those who venerate you on earth.

Our Father, Hail Mary, Glory be...

The Seven Joys and Sorrows of Joseph

There is a mediaeval Carol, 'Joys Seven', which enumerates the joys of Mary as:

"To see the blessed Jesus Christ when He was first her Son;
To see her own Son Jesus Christ to make the lame to go;
To see her own Son Jesus Christ to make the blind to see;
To see her own Son Jesus Christ to read the Bible o'er;
To see her own Son Jesus Christ to bring the dead alive;
To see her own Son Jesus Christ upon the crucifix;
To see her own Son Jesus Christ to wear the crown
    of Heaven."

Traditional piety has thought of Joseph in a similar context and variously identified his joys and sorrows.

Joys	Sorrows
His Betrothal to Mary	The pains of his own annunciation
News of the Incarnation	The journey to the census
The birth of his foster-son	Failure to find lodgings
The adoration of the Shepherds and the Magi	Gabriel's warnings
Finding Jesus in the Temple	The flight into Egypt
Teaching and nurturing Jesus	The loss of Jesus
Re-union with his family in Heaven.	Simeon's warning of Mary's sorrows.

"Remember, O most chaste spouse of the Virgin Mary, that never was it known that any one who implored your help and sought your intercession, was left unassissted. Full of confidence in your power, I rush to you for protection. Despise not, O Foster-father of the Redeemer, my humble supplication, but in your goodness hear and answer me." (*Memorare to St Joseph*)

"Gracious Saint Joseph, Patron of the universal Church, defend this mystic bark against the waves of heresy and the storms of hatred which assail it. Protect our Holy Father the Pope, and grant that all nations will become united to the See and teachings of Peter, so that there may be but one flock and one true Shepherd."

"To you, O Blessed Joseph, we have recourse in our tribulations and, while imploring the aid of your most holy spouse, we confidently invoke your patronage also. By the love which united you to the Immaculate Virgin Mother of God, and the fatherly affection with which you embraced the Infant Jesus, we beseech you to look graciously on the inheritance which He has purchased by His blood, and to help us in our necessities by your powerful intercession. As you once rescued the Child Jesus from mortal danger, now defend the Church of God from her enemies. Shield each one with your constant patronage so that, by imitating your example and with your help, we may lead a good life, die a

holy death, and come to everlasting happiness in heaven."
(*From an indulgenced prayer for October*).

"O Blessed Joseph, such are your virtues and the power of your intercession with God, that you are worthy to be venerated, loved and invoked before all the Saints. In the presence of Jesus who chose you as His father on earth, and of Mary who accepted you as her husband, I ask you to be my advocate with both, and my protector and father. I place my soul and body in your special protection. To you I entrust all my hopes and consolations, pains and miseries, my whole life and its last moment so that, through your holy intercession and your merits, everything I do may be in accordance with the will of your Divine Foster-Son." (*Consecration to Saint Joseph*).

Litany of Saint Joseph

Lord have mercy on us (2),
Christ have mercy on us (2),
Lord have mercy on us (2).
Christ hear us, Christ graciously hear

God the Father of Heaven
Have mercy on us
God the Son,
Redeemer of the world

Have mercy on us
God the Holy Spirit
Have mercy on us
Holy Mary

Pray for us
Saint Joseph
Pray for us
Renowned descendant
of David
Pray for us
Light of Patriarchs
Pray for us
Spouse of the Mother
of God
Pray for us
Chaste guardian of
the Virgin
Pray for us
Foster-father of the
Son of God
Pray for us
Diligent protector of Christ
Pray for us
Head of the Holy Family
Pray for us
Joseph most just
Pray for us
Joseph most chaste
Pray for us
Joseph most prudent
Pray for us

Joseph most courageous
Pray for us
Joseph most obedient
Pray for us
Joseph most faithful
Pray for us
Mirror of patience
Pray for us
Model of workers
Pray for us
Glory of home life
Pray for us
Guardian of virgins
Pray for us
Pillar of families
Pray for us
Solace of the wretched
Pray for us
Hope of the sick
Pray for us
Patron of the dying
Pray for us
Terror of demons
Pray for us
Protector of Holy Church
Pray for us

Lamb of God who takes away the sins of the world,
spare us O Lord.
Lamb of God who takes away the sins of the world,
graciously hear us O Lord.
Lamb of God who takes away the sins of the world,
have mercy on us

V. He made him the Lord of his household,
R. And prince over all his possessions.

O God, who in your ineffable providence chose blessed Joseph to be the spouse of Your most holy Mother, grant, we beseech You, that we may have him for our intercessor in Heaven, whom we venerate on earth. Through Christ Our Lord, Amen.

Hymns

"Joseph, wise ruler of God's earthly household,
nearest of all men to the heart of Jesus,
Be still a father, lovingly providing for us his brethren."
(*Liturgy of the Hours, 19th March*)

"Joseph, the Scriptures love to trace the glories
   of thy kingly line;
Yet no successor of thy race,
   no long posterity was thine –
Of her the everlasting spouse who must a Virgin ever be,

The faithful ruler of his house who owns no fatherhood
  in thee."
(*R. A. Knox, 1888-1957*)

"Joseph, pure spouse of that immortal Bride
who shines in ever-virgin glory bright,
Through all the Christian climes thy praise be sung,
through all the realms of light.
Thee, when amazed concern for thy betrothed
had filled thy righteous spirit with dismay,
An angel visited, and, with blest words,
    scattered thy fears away.

Thine arms embraced thy Maker newly born,
with Him to Egypt's desert didst thou flee;
Him in Jerusalem didst seek and find,
oh grief, oh joy to thee.
Not until after death their blissful crown others obtain;
but unto thee was given,
In thine own lifetime, to enjoy thy God as do the blest
  in Heaven."
(*17th Cent. Tr. E. Caswell, 1814-78*).

"Friend of the angels in Paradise still,
helpless humanity's refuge from ill,
Joseph, the worship and strength of our days,
graciously hear us who sing to thy praise.

Chosen thou wert by thy Maker's decree
spotless virginity's bridegroom to be;
Thee the Eternal his father would call,
steward on earth of his bounty to all."
(*'Caelitum Joseph', 17th Cent. Tr. R. A. Knox*).

"Whoe'er would live a holy life, whoe'er in joy would die,
Let him Saint Joseph's aid implore and on his help rely.
He Jesus Foster-father was, the Virgin Mother's spouse;
Just, faithful, pure, whatever he asks,
    their grateful love allows.
Adorer of the Child Divine, Consoler in His flight,
When lost, he seeks Him tearfully
    and finds Him with delight.
The mighty Maker of the world on him for
    bread depends;
To him th'eternal Father's Son His will submissive bends.
When death drew nigh he saw with joy the dawn
    of heaven's day;
With Jesus, Mary, by his side he gently passed away."
(*'Quicumque Sanus Vivere', La Sallian Responses in
honour of Saint Joseph and asking for his spirit and
assistance in the Christian Education of children.*)

THE FEASTS

The Betrothal of Our Lady to Saint Joseph

Formerly 23rd January

Though this Feast no longer appears in the Roman Calendar, the liturgy remains a rich source of doctrine, and lifts minds and hearts to prayer. The Collect asks God to give peace to all for whom the birth of Mary's Child is the beginning of salvation, and adds, "Let the merits of Saint Joseph, your holy mother's husband, assist and, through his intercession, may we be granted that which we could never win through our own unaided efforts."

The Reading is from the Letter to the Romans (1:1-6)

St Paul writes as "a servant of Christ Jesus who has been called to be an apostle, and specially chosen to preach the Good News that God promised long ago through His prophets in the Scriptures. This news is about the Son of God who, according to the human nature He took, was a descendant of David and who, in the order of the Spirit of holiness that was declared in Him, was proclaimed Son of God in all His power through His resurrection from the dead…" In these few words he has assembled the articles of early Christian faith: the purpose and mission of the apostolate, allegiance to Our Lord who is descended from the House of David, the proof of His divine nature through the Resurrection, and His glorification. He takes for granted that his readers are aware that Davidic descent was through Joseph (*Mt* 1:1ff), and does not expand on the subject. He remembers the prophets like Jeremiah who spoke of God with authority and certainty. "See the days are coming – it is the Lord who speaks – when I will raise a virtuous branch for David, who will reign as true king and be wise, practising honesty and integrity in the land." (*Jr 3:5 and see also Samuel, First Reading, 19th March*).

The Gospel: Mt 1:18-21
(See 'Annunciation and Visitation' p. 19 above)

The Offertory prayer is one of homage to the Lord who is entreated to preserve His gifts within us, "in answer to the prayers of blessed Joseph who espoused the Mother of Jesus Christ our Lord and, in whose worshipful memory, the dedicated offerings are presented with praise and thanksgiving."

The Solemnity of Saint Joseph

*Husband of the Blessed Virgin Mary, Guardian of the
Child Jesus and Patron of Christ's Universal Church*

19th March

"The Lord has put His faithful servant in charge of His
household." (*Entrance Antiphon*).

In a reading from the Second Book of Kings, Samuel, the
first prophet after Moses and the last of the great judges, tells
how the Lord promised David, "When your days are ended
and you are laid to rest with your ancestors, I will preserve the
offspring of your body after you and make his sovereignty
secure. It is he who will build a house for my name and I will
make his royal throne secure forever." (7:4-5, 12-14, 16).
God's mercies to David culminated in a new covenant of
grace, and the offspring of the royal house includes Joseph
and Christ in whom it finds its highest fulfilment.

The Gospel: Mt 1:16, 18-21, 24
(See 'Annunciation and Visitation' p. 19 above)

In the Preface, the Church thanks God for Saint Joseph, the
'just man', the wise and loyal servant whom He placed at
the head of His family, a sentiment evocative of Joseph's
Old Testament namesake in whom Pharaoh placed complete
trust. "With a husband's love, he cherished Mary, the Virgin
Mother of God. With fatherly care he watched over Jesus
Christ who was conceived by the power of the Holy Spirit."

Reflection

Saint Bernardine of Siena reminds the Church that special thanks and veneration are accorded to Joseph who is wonderfully placed to intercede for us with Jesus and Mary. "Whenever divine grace selects someone to receive a particular grace, or some especially favoured position, all the gifts for his state are given to that person, and enrich him abundantly. This is true of Joseph, the reputed father of Our Lord and the true husband of the Queen of the world and of the Angels. He was chosen by God to be the faithful foster-parent and guardian of the most precious treasures of God, His Son and His Spouse, a task he carried out so faithfully that the Lord said to him, 'Good and faithful servant, enter into the joy of your Lord.' Joseph may be compared to the whole Church. It was through, and in obedience to, him that Christ chose to enter the world in an appropriate way. If the Church is in debt to Mary through whom it is able to receive Christ, then it also owes Joseph special thanks and veneration. He marks the closing of the Old Testament, and the dignity of the prophets and patriarchs achieves its promised fulfilment in him who alone possessed in the flesh what God, in His goodness, promised to them over and over again. It is certain that Christ, now in a complete and perfect way, accords to Joseph in Heaven the same intimacy, respect and honour which He showed to him as a father during His human life." (*Office of Readings for the Feast*).

The Solemnity of Saint Joseph
Confessor and Patron of the Universal Church

Third Wednesday after Easter

Though this Feast no longer figures in the Roman Calendar, its liturgy remains relevant and inspiring.

The Lesson is taken from Genesis 49:22-26
(Trans R. A. Knox)

"A fruitful bough is Joseph; a fruitful bough, and fair to view; His branches run over the wall. Sorely his enemies harrass him with the darts they throw, unrelenting in their hatred, but his bow rests in the strength that does not fail him; the power of the God who rules in Jacob gives free play to hand and arm. From Joseph one shall arise, who will be the shepherd and corner stone of Israel. The God of thy father shall bring thee aid; the Almighty shall bless thee with all the blessings that lie stored in heaven above or in the depth beneath us, all the blessings that enrich breast and womb. This blessing which thy father gives thee draws strength from all the blessings which his own fathers bequeathed; they shall not cease till he comes, whom the everlasting hills await. May they all rest on Joseph's head, rest on his brow, who is separated like a Nazarite, from his brethren."

Reflection

The description of Joseph in the Old Testament is an anticipation of the heroic character of Our Lord's foster-father. Certainly, the 'just man' and spouse of the Mother of God, is like a young fruit-tree by a spring whose tendrils reach over obstacles. With the support of the same Mighty One who helped his ancestor, Jacob, and through the power of the Shepherd of Israel, he is unflinching in the face of persecution and the assaults of those who seek to harm his precious charge. The blessings of the eternal hills, fixed and immovable from the beginning of the world descend upon his crown, so he is rightly called a prince among his brethren. Like a vigorous vine, his strong arms provide protection and sustenance to Him who is the expectation of the nations. The theme is continued in the Gospel in which, at the beginning of Jesus' mission, God the Father acknowledges His only Son, and divine co-equal, whom He has entrusted to Saint Joseph. "Now when all the people had been baptised and while Jesus, after his own baptism was at prayer, heaven opened and the Holy Spirit descended on him in bodily shape, like a dove. And a voice came from heaven, 'You are my Son, the Beloved; my favour rests on you... Jesus was about thirty years old, being the son, as it was thought, of Joseph." (*Lk* 3:21-23).

The Holy Family of Jesus, Mary and Joseph

Sunday within the Octave of Christmas or 31st December

In this Holy Family, God the Father's love gives us an order and framework for life on earth. The family is the foundation unit of human society and its well-being. It mirrors the relationship with God in which love and obedience lead to fulfilment, and demonstrates to the world God's love which He reveals in Christ. Today, the Church celebrates the Feast of the Holy Family and "meditates with profound reverence on the holy life led in the House at Nazareth by Jesus the Son of God, Mary His Mother and Joseph the 'just man'… There is a lesson in family life… May Nazareth teach us what family life is, its commandment of love, its austere and simple beauty and its sacred and inviolable character. Let us learn from Nazareth that the formation received at home is gentle and irreplaceable. Let us learn the importance of the social order." (*Pope Paul VI, 'Marialis Cultus', 1964*).

God's desire that marriage and family should be the context in which husband, wife, and children should flourish, finds expression in His fourth Commandment when He tells children to honour their fathers and mothers, and all legitimate authority. The benefit of the individual and the progress of society is interdependent, and inseparable form healthy family relationships within the sacred guardianship of marriage. Those who value "the domestic church" appreciate that fostering an exchange of loving care is their duty as partners, parents and spouses concerned for their children's education in faith, prayer and all the virtues, as well as their physical development. In return, the children's loving respect for their parents preserves harmony in the family home, and it is "a wise son who hears his father's instruction." (*Pr* 3:1). St Luke says as much when referring to the way in which Jesus matured physically and spiritually as God intended. At Nazareth, He was obedient to Mary and Joseph and grew "in wisdom, in stature, and in favour with God." The deep marital love between Joseph and Mary reflects God's love for every one of the children He creates, and is most perfectly shown in Joseph's foster-son who so loves His Bride, the Church, that "He sacrificed Himself for her to make her holy. He made her clean by washing her in water with a form of words, so that when He took her to Himself she would be glorious…holy and faultless." (*Ep* 5:25-27). Joseph's close and loving relationship with the young Jesus balances long hours of work, as provider and protector, with the benefits of a father's intimate involvement in the upbringing of children. On His part, Jesus shows filial respect and a true docility which, as children emulate, they will see as a source not only of peace but of their own well-adjusted development. (*cf.* '*Pastoral Constitution on the Church in the World of Today* 47:1).

After the Entrance Antiphon has remembered how the shepherds went to Bethlehem and found Mary, Joseph and the Baby lying in a manger, the Collect praises God who crowned the goodness of creation with the family of man. He sent His Son to dwell in time and conform to the laws of life in the world. In the sanctity of human love and, with awareness of the value of family life, we pray that we are helped to live in peace and come to share God's eternal life.

The reading from the Book of Ecclesiasticus, though predating the Nativity by two centuries, is relevant to family life in every age as parents share in God's act of creation, the transmission of life and the moulding of personality. The tenderness they show their offspring, especially when they can do nothing for themselves, is a manifestation of the love God has for all His children and from which their own springs. Children will have their own opportunity to be creative when they see their parents' powers diminish with age, and they recognise the wonders God has wrought through their relationships. "The Lord honours the father in his children and upholds the rights of a mother over her sons. Whoever respects his father is like someone amassing a fortune. Whoever respects his father will be happy with children of his own and he shall be heard on the day when he prays. Long life comes to him who honours his father; he who sets his mother at ease is showing obedience to the Lord." (*Si* 3:2-6, 12-14).

The Responsorial Psalm 127 counts the blessings of a home-life in which the essential nature of relationship with God is acknowledged. It is addressed to the father of the household and, in this case, the Church speaks to Joseph in whose family Jesus chose to be a child. "O blessed are those who fear the Lord and walk in His ways! By the labour of your hands you shall eat; you will be happy and prosper. Your wife like a fruitful vine in the heart of the house; your children like shoots of the olive around your table. Indeed thus shall be blessed the man who fears the Lord. May the Lord bless you from Zion all the days of your life." Joseph is the good father who, with his wife provides for the spiritual and physical needs of his family. Mary is the fruitful vine, the Mother of a Child who is like the olive shoot which brings health and vigour to the world. God blesses such a father whose fidelity is rewarded with peace and prosperity in Jerusalem, the figure of the heavenly city.

In his Epistle to the Colossians (3:12-21), St Paul understands how, in the Holy Family, God has given us a framework for personal life in a civilised, caring society. He gives his own expression to the family as the foundation of society, and the reflection of our relationship with God in which loving obedience leads to fulfilment. "You are God's chosen race, His saints; He loves you and you should be clothed in sincere compassion, kindness and humility, gentleness and patience. Bear with one another;

forgive each other as soon as a quarrel begins. The Lord
has forgiven you, now you must do the same. Teach and
advise one another in all wisdom…and never say or do any
thing except in the name of the Lord Jesus, giving thanks
to God the Father through Him."

*Gospel: Mt 2:13-15, 19-23. (See 'After the Nativity: the
Escape to Egypt; from Egypt to Nazareth' pp. 34-38).*

"Lord Jesus we adore you, Son of the living God. You
became Son to a human family and lived under the
authority of Mary and Joseph. Teach us to walk the path
of humility. Your Parents kept in their hearts all that You
said and did. May we learn from their example the spirit
of contemplation. Help us to see our own labour as a
sharing of Yours." (*Intercessions of the Feast, adapted,
Liturgy of the Hours*).

"God our Father, in the Holy Family of Nazareth, you
have given us the true model of the Christian home. Grant
that, by following Jesus, Mary and Joseph in their love
for each other and in the example of their family life, we
may come to join you in your home in peace and joy."
(*Evening Prayer, Liturgy of the Hours*).

Saint Joseph the Worker

1st May

The Collect acknowledges that God, the Creator, expects
us, like Joseph, to develop and use the gifts we have
received for the benefit of others. A reading from Genesis
recalls God's command to every man and woman He
creates to be fruitful, to fill the earth, subdue it, and use the
Sabbath rest which He has ordained for His worship and
our refreshment in the work of life. In his letter to the
Colossians, St Paul recommends that, whatever our work
is, we put our hearts into it as if it were for the Lord, and
do everything in His name. An Intercession in the Liturgy
of the Hours asks Him who has given man authority over
the work of His hands and an invitation to share the work
of Creation, to help him accept the responsibility of
working for His glory and for the benefit of humanity. The
Gospel tells of Our Lord's own work of teaching in the
synagogues, His mission to the people, and His being
recognised as "the carpenter's son." (*Gn* 1:26-23; *Col* 3:17;
Mt 13:54-58).

Among the prayers which the Church uses, two in
particular sublimate the daily routine of work and give
new meaning to mundane tasks which are directed
towards salvation.

"Lord, You have brought us to the beginning of this
day. Protect us with Your power so that we will not fall

into any sin, and that all our thoughts and actions will be directed to the performance of Your justice."

"O Jesus, through the Immaculate Heart of Mary, I offer you all my prayers, works, joys and sufferings of this day in union with the intentions of Your Divine Heart in the Holy Mass." (*Morning Offering*).

Reflection: Work as a means of Salvation.

The Industrial Revolution posed new problems for society, not least of which were the appalling conditions in which many workers had to earn a living. The social and political influence with which the Church had long been associated seemed to have become distant from their circumstances, and Pope Leo XIII was sensitive to their emerging alienation exarcebated by widening class divisions. In 1891, in his first, major social encyclical 'Of New Things: On the Conditions of the Working Person' (*'Rerum Novarum', 1891*), he defended workers' rights to form trade unions, to work in an humane environment, and be paid a just wage. He emphasised the Church's right and responsibility to relate her teaching to the well-being of all people during their life on earth, to identify existing problems, recommend remedies, and offer solutions. This responsible mission is not the sole preserve of the clerical hierarchy, and lay people, by the exercise of moral conscience, are equally involved in ensuring that the policies and decisions of the state are compatible with the teaching of the Church on justice and human rights.

During the next hundred years, a series of Papal, conciliar, and episcopal pronouncements followed Pope Leo's encyclical. These included, 'Forty Years After' (*'Quadragesimo Anno', Pius XI, 1931*), 'The Eightieth Anniversary' (*'Octogesima Adveniens', Paul VI, 1971*) and 'The Redeemer of Mankind' (*'Redemptor Hominis', 1979*), wherein Pope John Paul II, in his very first encyclical, concerned himself with the dignity of the human being, the Church's preferential option for the poor, and the importance of adhering to her social teaching which has its source in the Gospel. Two years later in 'On Human Work' (*'Laborem Exercens'*), he explained that work has a spiritual dimension which stems from an acceptance of God's invitation to participate in His continuing work of creation, and he called for renewed acknowledgement of, and support for, the dignity of the human family throughout the world, whose rights must not be ignored or violated. As a centenary memorial to *'Rerum Novarum'*, he wrote his encyclical 'The Hundredth Year' (*'Centessimus Annus'*), to reaffirm that the Gospel's social message was not just theory but a plan of positive action. He insisted that social teaching was intrinsic to evangelisation, and, though the Church might refrain from actually proposing programmes, her social teaching offered a necessary and ideal direction for progress.

Meanwhile, the Second Vatican Council (1962-65) had articulated the Church's mission to promote and guide attitudes towards the work of one's calling. Holiness is attained by fidelity to daily responsibilities and when undertaken in the spirit of faith, these bring men and women closer to God as they respond to the resources and values of the Creation which He has revealed. He makes human beings in His own image to share His work of creation, and their labours become holy as they honour Him by using the gifts and capabilities He has bestowed. The achievements and efforts of human beings are manifestations of the greatness of Him who made them, and the service of life is a demonstration of the loving care for the world by Him from whom all good things come. The Council Fathers concluded that there is no distinction between the profession of faith and the practice of daily life in all its details, nor is there any tension between professional and social activity on the one hand and religious life on the other. It is is in the conditions of life, with its duties and responsibilities, that humanity, sustained by faith, and accepting everything as coming from God's hands, grows holy and pleasing to Him.

In the seventeenth century, St John Baptist de la Salle gave his congregation this succinct and felicitous advice: "It is a good rule of conduct to make no distinction between the matters proper to one's state of life and the advancement of salvation and perfection… One will never work better for one's salvation, nor acquire greater perfection than by accomplishing the duties of daily employment when these are carried out in view of God's intentions." The Second Vatican Council concurred that apostolic works, prayers, endeavours, the daily work of vocation, recreation, troubles patiently endured, carrying one's share of Christ's Cross, all are offered as part of the perfect Sacrifice He continues to make to His Father.

In the economy of salvation, God wills that each individual and collective enterprise should enhance the quality and condition of mortal life. Because He makes men and women in His own image, He is honoured when the earth is filled and subdued, and when the rule of holiness and justice established. He wants His children to sanctify themselves by working for their own and their families' benefit, and using their energies for the good of society by an honest, responsible stewardship of His Creation. His own creative activity is witnessed in industrial progress and human achievement when it is directed to the well-being of humanity as a sign of His loving care. When progress is inspired by justice, social order, and the exercise of talents given by God to further the social fulfilment of the race, it is in harmony with His Divine Plan. "The Christian finds in human work a small part of Christ's cross and accepts it in the same spirit of redemption in which He accepted His cross for us. Thanks to the light which penetrates us from His resurrection, we find in work a glimmer of new life, of new good." ('*Of Human Work*' and cf. *Gn 1:20-27; Ws 9:2-3; 'Dogmatic Constitution on the Church' (Lumen Gentium 39, 41-43); Pastoral Constitution on the Church in the World of Today (Gaudium et Spes 41-43, 63ff); Catechism of the Catholic Church 2426-8*).

St Peter tells us that because Jesus has made Himself one with us, we are participants in His new and holy priesthood which offers all the sacrifices which He has now made acceptable to His Father, and we are living stones in the construction of a spiritual house. (*1 P* 2:4-9). Our Lord is "the trustworthy High Priest", not only in ritual but in every moment and aspect of His life. Because He shares our humanity, He consecrates every aspect of human existence, including life's routine, and His presence makes all things holy, so that His brothers and sisters are able to sanctify the world. In Baptism He welcomes us to share in the establishment of God's Kingdom, and His love, at work in our hearts, dignifies the mundane and sublimates what seems ordinary. Such a thought helps overcome feelings of inadequacy, especially when we read of the saints' wonderful exploits in their close association with Jesus. When He calls us with the "special grace of a good steward", it is as the person He created and whom He knows better than we know ourselves. Our best response is to walk to Him with confidence, happy that we have at our disposal the treasury of the Church, with all the merits and actions of Mary, Joseph, and the saints in the Mystical Body. (*cf. 1 P* 4:10-11).

Prayers as we wake up and contemplate the day ahead

"O Lord, You have brought me to the beginning of the day. Save me by Your power so that I may not fall into any sin. May everything I say, and all that I do, be directed to the performance of Thy justice, through Christ Our Lord." (*Prayer of the Church*).

"Lord, May everything I do begin with Your inspiration, continue with Your help, and reach conclusion under Your guidance." (*Prayer of the Church*)

"O Jesus, through the most pure heart of Mary, I offer you all my prayers, works, joys and sufferings of this day in union with the intentions of Thy Divine Heart in the Holy Mass." (*Morning Offering*).

ACKNOWLEDGEMENTS

The CTS gratefully acknowledges use of prayers, scripture quotations and hymns from:

The Jerusalem Bible (Darton, Longman and Todd, London 1974)

The New Testament (Burns & Oates and Washbourne Ltd, London 1948)

The Divine Office (Collins, London 1974)

Papal Documents (Catholic Truth Society, London)

Westminster Hymnal (Burns & Oates and Washbourne, London 1948)

Catholic Commentary on the Holy Scripture (Thomas Nelson and Sons, London 1951)

The Psalms, A New Translation (The Grail, England, published by Collins, 1963)

Catechism of the Catholic Church (Geoffrey Chapman, London 1994).